HE DO THE GAY MAN IN DIFFERENT VOICES

STEPHEN S. MILLS

SiblingRivalryPress
Alexander, Arkansas
www.siblingrivalrypress.com

He Do the Gay Man in Different Voices

Copyright © 2012 by Stephen S. Mills

Front cover photograph and author photograph by Stephen S. Mills. Used by permission.

Cover design by Mona Z. Kraculdy.

All rights reserved. No part of this book may be reproduced or republished without written consent from the publisher, except by reviewers who may quote brief excerpts in connection with a review in a newspaper, magazine, or electronic publication; nor may any part of this book be reproduced, stored in a retrieval system, or transmitted in any form, or by any means be recorded without written consent of the publisher.

Sibling Rivalry Press, LLC
13913 Magnolia Glen Drive
Alexander, AR 72002

www.siblingrivalrypress.com

ISBN: 978-1-937420-08-6

Library of Congress Control Number: 2011944777

First Sibling Rivalry Press Edition, March 2012

For Dustin

CONTENTS

Part I

Warning: In Case of Rapture This Vehicle Will Be Unmanned / 11

Sex Education / 14

Missing You While Watching *Misery* / 17

Iranian Boys Hanged for Sodomy, July 2005 / 19

Night Watch / 21

Fisting You for the First Time on the Day "Don't Ask, Don't Tell" is Repealed / 23

He Do the Gay Man in Different Voices / 26

The Ghost of Little Edie Beale Meets Me in a Gay Bar / 35

Imagining Your Penis in Blue After Watching *Watchmen* / 38

My Father Calls With More Bad News / 40

Against Our Better Judgment We Plan a Trip to Iran / 43

The Anatomy of a Hate Crime / 44

Part II

An Experiment in How to Become Someone Else Who Isn't Moving Anymore / 49

Part III

In a Porn Store / 69

There is No Nickolay Petrov / 71

September 21, 1991 / 74

Just Add Water, Scene 2 / 76

$5,000 / 77

My Boyfriend Tells My Parents I'm Writing to a Gay Porn Star in Prison / 79

Lines From a Prison Letter / 80

$10,000 / 82

I Tell Edmon He Writes Better Than My Students / 84

A History of Blood / 86

I Dream Edmon Escapes / 88

Sitting in My Cubical I Reconsider a Porn Career / 90

After Watching *Capote* I Decide Not to Send These Poems to Edmon / 92

You've Gone Silent / 93

Imagining You in a Prison Photograph / 94

HE DO THE GAY MAN IN DIFFERENT VOICES

Part I

WARNING: IN CASE OF RAPTURE
THIS VEHICLE WILL BE UNMANNED

When Michael died in a car accident speeding
home from his girlfriend's—a fight about money
or babies or both—I wondered what his body
looked like crumpled in the rubble of the cement
wall he crashed into—I was fourteen. His parents
donated his organs. Organs packed in coolers
and shipped off as last minute stays of execution.
They said God had a plan: one life gone, many lives
saved. Nick was the first atheist I ever knew.
He didn't mind I was religious when he shoved
my head into the pillow and moved inside me
on the waterbed I inherited from my grandmother
after she collapsed on a cold February morning.
I remember the jostle of the water as he pumped
his still-growing hips into me. He stopped coming
over when my mother found a condom in my desk
drawer, and he found a boy with tattoos, a pierced
tongue, a plaid shirt tied at his waist. It was the 1990s.
Everyone was cooler than me. Then there was a girl,
freshmen year of college, who drowned in her car
when it veered off an icy Indiana road. Her body
trapped inside a steel coffin. Classmates prayed.
Said she was in a better place. The chapel buzzed
as I stayed in my dorm room chatting online with boys
who promised big dicks and tight chests if I was willing
to drive sixty miles in any direction. Who was in more
denial? The only girl I ever kissed worked at church
camps in the summer. Taught kids how to make God
eyes out of popsicle sticks and yarn. Made me go
to church with her. Made me stand in circles
while people cried and swayed with the spirit. A spirit
that made her say we couldn't go all the way.

I faked disappointment and jerked off in the privacy
of the communal bathroom I shared with sweaty
jocks. Then there was the night in the Wal-Mart
parking lot when a man in a white pickup chased
my old Buick around after I accidently cut him off.
The police said there was nothing they could do.
He had committed no crime, as of yet. *Call me when
he hits you*. He revved his engine, sped at me, over
and over again. On his back glass he proclaimed
his love of Jesus Christ, his NRA membership,
and his Bush support. Finally, he gave up on slamming
into me, got out, walked to the front of the store,
and paced—waiting to beat the living shit out of me.
All part of a plan, I suppose. Instead, I went home
to the boy in my bed. The one who liked to play
in the hair of my body. Brushing against my ass,
my legs, my chest. By the time Drew got hit and killed
by a car, outside Chicago, while riding his bike to protest
our dependency on foreign oil, God was dead. I cried
into a boy's shoulder and then went out to dinner.
The living must eat. I drove the car extra careful,
eyes wide, searching for the next killer, the next victim.
Then today, I heard about you, how an SUV hit your wheel-
chair as you crossed the street on campus. The same
street you crossed so many times before, but today
was your last. I won't say we were friends. I hate
when the living proclaim an untrue bond with the dead.
We were acquaintances, once peers, fellow writers.
I don't imagine your body on that hot August blacktop,
though I can picture the cracks in the frame of your seat,
your bag tossed, paper blowing in the hot Florida wind,
and I can see the young girl who hit you. Probably
a college student excited for the new term. A Southern
girl with strong faith and a good sense of right
and wrong, but I wonder if she thought of fleeing,
of never coming back, of never knowing the end result.

You don't die, if she doesn't stay. People go missing
every day. But she didn't leave, and nothing could save
you. Not her prayers or yours lost somewhere inside you.
Now, she gets to live with the weight of killing you,
with the fact that if she'd been 30 seconds faster,
she would've missed you, flown right by you—still
on the sidewalk. She might've caught you in the corner
of her eye, might've smiled, waved, gone on her way
as you wheeled safely across the street, alive for another
day, unaware of just how lucky and thankful you should be.

SEX EDUCATION

It was spring in Indiana when that man raped
the gray-haired lady who went to worship
with us. The one who wore purple skirts

and sturdy tan shoes like loaves of day-old bread
my father brought home for us. The man snuck
into her house, tied her with a phone cord, raped her

while her dog howled in the bathroom—trapped,
waterless, and scared. For days my parents
whispered over dinner boiling on the stove

and by the next week we all felt the icy current
of my mother's fear wash over us when I left
the door unlocked on my way to the bus,

her alone inside. But by the end of May the woman
was back in her pew, an unshakable Quaker,
firm in the belief that silence heals everything.

I examined her for bruises she hid in floppy sweaters
until summer came and melted the victim from her skin,
exposing the remains of his fingers still smudged on her

like a painter's thumb on the back of the canvas.

****

It was the same year they took our fingers to ink,
smeared them on blue note cards, marked
with our name and picture. Placed them in files

meant to save us. It was after that little boy
vanished. The one my mother dreamt of finding
stuck in a clothes rack at J.C. Penney,

or buried beneath the tomatoes in the grocery aisle,
still breathing. The boy looked a lot like me,
blond hair, blue eyes, when they found him

in that cornfield, his anus bloodied, his nails full
of earth. But my parents believed in fingerprints,
in their ability to keep me from disappearing

into the hands of men who can't control
their fascination with the way color leaves
the body. Men I'd take to bed, years later,

my feet bound in their neckties, scarves, handcuffs.

****

In school that fall, Mr. Brock nervously taught the boys
"reproduction" like a cold science, as if he knew

some of us would become monsters. Our desires
lurking in our groins like a disease we might succumb to.

Our blue plastic chairs scooted across the hardwood
floor of the gymnasium as the girls sat Indian style

across the hall in the dimmed cafeteria, watching a film
on the mysteries of bloody panties and sore chests.

The boys got diagrams: blueprints of bodies
meant only to produce bald, screaming babies each time

our middles touched a girl's. Mine never did.

****

By October the rapist was caught. His mustache and beady
eyes on the front page of every Midwest newspaper:

six counts of rape, four of first-degree murder. *She's lucky,*
my parents spoke in voices loud enough to hear,

but I knew better. Knew she must have his baby growing
inside her, but hoped it would stay forever trapped in her belly

like her dog in the bathroom on that spring night, or her
throat in his hands, the color rushing from her face.

MISSING YOU WHILE WATCHING *MISERY*

I'm the writer, but it's you I imagine tied to the bed,
legs unable to move, trapped by a madwoman
like all the madwomen of literature that have come
before her. I can see you planning your escape,
wheeling around the house, frantically storing knives
in your arm sling, and it would be just like you
to knock over that penguin and not think to place
it facing the correct direction. Of course, it's hard
to picture you in that hobbling scene that makes
everyone so uncomfortable, but I can understand
not wanting to lose a man, and sometimes love hurts.
In reality, you are visiting your parents in Indiana,
and I'm here in Florida in the heat of summer
missing you and watching Annie Wilkes force Paul
to write another novel, to bring his heroine back
to life like I bring you to life here on this page,
even though you are 800 miles away and I have no
idea what you are actually doing or who you are with.
Two weeks is a long time for men who have spent
almost every single day together for nearly seven years—
we have a life, a routine, an intimacy in this apartment
where Paul types away on our big-screen TV.
It's enough to make the sane insane, because everybody
needs somebody. I almost sympathize with Annie
and her pig (a pet I've always wanted) or maybe
it's just my love of Kathy Bates coming through.
Love is love, even if it's forced, or confused,
or one-sided. On the telephone we proclaim how much
we miss the other, rattle off all the dirty things
we want to do to the other's body, and how lonely
beds can be, which makes us feel silly, codependent,
like lost boys who will never grow up or find
their way back home. Thankfully, we have planes,

tickets, schedules. Annie is bloody now. Paul
just whacked her with his typewriter (the one missing
the letter N), but you know she's not dead yet,
because madness doesn't end that quickly. She's got
a few more minutes, a few more blows before life
gives up on her. Did she ever really stand a chance?
Do we? When you return, I'll take you to our bed,
use the straps we bought at the sex store, tie your legs
in the air, and make you mine. This we will call sexy.
This we will call love.

IRANIAN BOYS HANGED FOR SODOMY, JULY 2005

We have their last photograph,
a magazine cutout of the blind-
folded boys, with nooses round
their necks and masked men
behind. Men with thick hands,
hands that keep everything
in order, everyone blind.

We let the picture drift around
the apartment like an omen
that will one day make perfect
sense. Some mornings I stick it
on the bathroom mirror before
you shave, the next you have it
on the fridge or tucked inside
my *O'Hara Collected*. Some nights
I slip it in a shoebox marked
"private" and forget we ever cut it

out, but by the following evening
it's under our mattress as we make
love. Each time I thrust into you,
I'm thrusting into them, creasing
their boyish bodies, one only 16.
On Sunday morning I ask you
if you think the Iranian boys
loved each other like I love you

here in America where true love
must be complicated. You're sure
they did, believe being hanged together
reeks of romance, of epic novels,
and Hollywood love stories, but

I fear it's just a case of being
in the wrong place at the wrong time.

All I can see are two terrified boys,
hands bound, about to be hanged
for public view. And I need to know
if it was quick. If the rope did what
ropes are meant to do or if the boys
found freedom in the dark
of their twitching eyelids?

NIGHT WATCH

We stand by the window on patrol, searching
        for the maroon car we've been warned about.
We know it contains a 16-year-old on a rampage,
        having already killed his parents.

A boy who might, now, be heading to this small
        college in the woods of Indiana to kill
his brother—his last remaining family member.

My roommate and I have *turned down the lights*,
        as he says in his Pakistani accent,
in my country I've had many lightless nights
        like this, playing, what do you call it here?

Hide and seek? *Yes, I'd play with the neighbor boys,*
        our families packed into one house, waiting
for the world to end. But this Midwest boy

isn't dropping bombs or blowing up the bus
        station. We don't even have a bus station
in this podunk Indiana town. Maybe I'm just
        embarrassed that American tragedy

has to be so cliché: the white, middle-class boy
        on a rampage because he hates
his privileged life, hates his working parents, fears

he'll never live up to the expectations of straight,
        white manhood. These are the same boys
who kill homeless people as a late-night game,
        taking baseball bats to worn faces.

Not as innocent as my roommate shouting boo
        in the dark to the girl he might one day fall
in love with. That is, if the world doesn't end.

Yes, my roommate enjoys the distraction, stays
        at the window while I go study by candlelight
for the morning's final exam—fall semester ending
        in four days. He stares down at the manicured

lawn, the frost on the leaves, and I think I catch
        a smile in the glass. A smile that says
even here among the Georgian-style buildings

there is suffering—there is death. Like the days
        he can't get out of bed, stays wrapped
in his golden comforter, doesn't shower, doesn't eat.
        Or the days I walk to the edge of campus

and imagine jumping into the Ohio River, floating off,
        starting over. Or the night I met a deer
coming out of the woods, how our eyes locked

as if to prove we were both alive. Though tonight,
        that deer might be dead. Shot by some
backwards hunter—hung and drained. Or maybe
        her guts were spilled across a winding, two-lane

road by a speeding car, a maroon car, a 16-year-old
        inside, his hands trembling, his throat bellowing
into the December air rushing through his open windows.

FISTING YOU FOR THE FIRST TIME ON THE DAY "DON'T ASK, DON'T TELL" IS REPEALED

You ask me to do it.
Buy the Crisco yourself.
Small tub. Non-butter
flavored. You come home
to me in bed, willingly
nervous. I tell you I will do
my best to forge this new
intimacy. You can't go back
once you've had your whole
fist inside someone.
I remove my ring.
The one you bought me
to prove how much you
love me, want to be with me.
Our attempt at normalcy.
I strip off my clothes.
Lay a towel on the bed.
Then we begin the art
of manipulating space.
Fists are really made
for punching holes
into walls, which we've
never done, not even in
our biggest, most brutal fights.
Though there is that dent
in the wall by the bed from
the night you pounded
it so hard because the bear
who lives next door
was having one of his
Mamma Mia sing-a-longs
at three o'clock in the morning.

But I don't even think
you used your fist
to make that dent,
probably just the palm
of your hand, which I've
used to slap you. Punching
seems so serious. Yes, fists
are made for punching
other boys in the face,
stomach, arm. But even these
fists we've avoided, both
never being in an actual fight
with grunts, blows, and blood.
Boys will be boys.
It seems as if our fists
were meant for a greater
purpose, a more challenging
one: the gentle stretching
of a lover. We are not
the same as boys who knock
holes into walls and faces.
Boys who can't control
their obsession with everything
ending in destruction.
This is about connecting
my body to yours. Halfway in,
I ask how it feels. Your eyes
tell me you're hungry
for the adventure of it,
for the story we will share
with friends over brunch
or drinks. And we will laugh,
smile, hold each other's hands
as we tell it. I keep going,
pushing against everything
your body has to give:

a tightness more powerful
than any boy's fist ever
thought about being.
It's the last bit that's the hardest,
or so they say on websites
with men in black leather
and swings hanging from bedroom
ceilings. It's the last move inward
that is both terrifying
and satisfying. Everything
warm and beating. Everything
hinging on my fingers being able
to bend down, scoop in,
form a fist inside you,
like a child you will never carry.

HE DO THE GAY MAN IN DIFFERENT VOICES

I.

It rained a lot that spring, making the days perfect
to spend in bed with him. His body just the right
temperature to keep us warm. In the morning,
I'd make eggs and coffee, serve them on a tray,
and think *how long can we keep this going before one of us
sneaks out at night never to return or sticks his head
in the oven?* Did it ever seem possible that the summer
would actually come? That the heat would overtake
everything? A hot summer that nearly killed
all the plants in the garden, in the flower beds,
in the pots on the porch full of wilting geraniums.
The city limited water use. Everyone feared fire.

At 12 I dressed in my mother's nylons, pulled
them as far as they could go, almost to my armpits
(still hairless). I stood in front of the bathroom's
floor length mirror watching my penis grow hard
against the nude fabric, stretching with each thought
of my own skin; my own boyish hands touching
my thighs, nipples, lips. I was a god bound
in the net of womanhood. When I was satisfied,
I slowly peeled them from my body, rolled them
into a ball, and buried them at the bottom
of the trashcan, which was taken out by my father
the following morning on his way to work. Weeks
later my mother shouted, while dressing
for a dinner party, *where are my good nylons?*
Angry at herself for losing them.

                                    But I like
to think of those days of rain, of him on his back
watching me, naked, by the window, then moving
toward him on that bed with the busted spring.

II.

It is May. Flowers are in bloom. May Day. Like when
I was 5 and made paper flowers at school to leave
on the doorstep of the neighbor lady with the German
shepherd and the bald husband who one day died
on her. Collapsed. Gone. Or was it a long slow fight?
I can't remember anymore, and does it really matter?
Slightly raised temperature. Sore throat. Coughing.
Lymph nodes swollen. Tea with honey. A red spot here
and there. Don't look too close. Don't ask too many
questions. People die every day—quietly, alone—
flowers or no flowers. I still have my hair. My teeth.
My lips, which sometimes still form a smile.

The man says I can't give blood. They don't want it.
It's tainted blood. Gay blood. Faggot blood.
*Too hard telling what you got, what sick disease hides
in your skin, in your veins, in that fucking brain of yours.*
Blood. So much blood. Like when they beat the shit
out of you. Leave you to die in the streets of Miami,
in the backwoods of the Midwest, or out West tied
to a fucking fence. They want our blood. Want it
spilled on the ground, soaking up the dirt, sticking
to their shoes, their pistols, their knives. Blood
is lifesaving—life-ending. *Sir, have you had sex
with another man since 1977? Yes or no?*

No. It's been more than "a man."

III.

My head is on his chest watching the smoke curl
from his mouth up to the cracked ceiling in this old
house, in this old town. We just made love.
No, we just fucked. Just met. In rural Indiana,
a good fuck is hard to find. Must travel. Must not
chicken out. Must be willing to go through
the window if a wife, mother, or roommate
abruptly comes home. He looks from his cigarette
to my eyes, asks: *would you fuck yourself?* I don't know
what he means, exactly. Can I fuck myself? No,
but I've seen a video of a guy who could, not very well,
but still got the job done. *I mean, if you could, like you
had two bodies, twins, only completely the same and control
over both.* He takes another puff. I've broken my rule:
no conversation with hookups, just sex. I've stayed
too long. Real life is seeping through the floorboards.
Before I know it the bed will be a field of corn ready
for harvest, ready for coarse hands that know years
of hard labor. Like my grandparents who worked
the land until their bodies became part of it,
until we buried them side by side in the crisp air
of October. They called me *the garden boy* for my love
of helping them till the dirt, pull the weeds, snap
the beans on the porch that creaked with each heavy
footstep. He's put out his cigarette, is waiting
for my answer, can't tell where I've gone, what secrets
hide in my skin, can't tell if he wants to know.
So I say, *I like watching myself fuck in the mirror,
is that the same thing?* He laughs, pulls the sheet off,
he's hard and wants to go again.

IV.

There was water. A reflection. A story about a man.
An obsession. I don't know all the details.
Don't need to. I've fallen into plenty of bodies
of water. Never have I drowned. Never have I not
resurfaced more beautiful than before. They call me
the damaged narcissist. But where's the damage?
I am perfection staring back at you, and you love me
because you can't ever have me.

I could hear his dress shoes on the pavement—
clip clop, like a horse in steady pursuit. Then
he was beside me. Glancing at me. Eyeing
the way my clothes hung on my boy—almost
man—frame. I was 16. *How was school?* He asked
like a dad who had heard it all before. *It was school.*
I could see the bulge in his pants. Feel the power
in mine. I knew he would do anything I wanted
just to be close to beauty, to youth. When he
finished sucking my cock in the backseat of his car,
he burst into tears, wanted to be held. I zipped
up, told him I had to get home to homework,
dinner, worried parents. As I opened the door,
I looked back just once at the pile of man
on the seat: wet, tie undone, pants still bulged.

The body fails us.
It can only take so much before
it breaks, sags, molds
into something that doesn't resemble
our old selves.
This is not me.
This body in the mirror.
Naked.
Skin and bone.

This man is dying.
This man cannot stop
bruising, bleeding, sinking
into himself.
This man is a fucking pussy,
even though he's never fucked one.
He's not me.
I am young.
I am beautiful.
I am the one all the boys want to take home,
want to fuck.
I am still here.
Trapped inside a body that has given itself up
to powers I don't believe in.
Yes, even in death, I believe in no god,
but myself.
I am more than this fading body,
which fails me over and over again.

V.

I know I'm not what you expected—a man now,
but a man who loves other men, who takes them
in his bed and makes them feel alive, gives them
pleasure, takes pleasure in return, but it's more
than that. It's about the morning after, about waking
to a body next to you, never feeling alone
or out of place again. Or sitting on the couch
and laughing at some stupid show with a beautiful
man in your arms, probably a show you are also
watching in your La-Z-Boy, half asleep and dreaming
of something better, or maybe something worse.
There's something about two men together—
an understanding that is ours to have, to hold on to.
I try to be a good man, to do what you taught me,

what you asked of me. Yes, the weather is a mystery.
The flowers do need rain.

                        It's last call in a bar
where a man hasn't stopped dancing with himself
in the mirror. No drink for him, just more dancing,
more meeting his own eye. Other men watch him,
mesmerized by his devotion to reflection. Others
pick out all the things wrong with him: his slightly
large ears, the crook of his nose, the style of his hair,
clothes, shoes. They wonder how he can stand
to stare at himself all night long. Why doesn't he
find them attractive, worthy of a look? It's last call.
Men are sick creatures and this bar has it all: the old
man who closes his eyes and sways with the music,
rarely opening them to see where he is. He's memorized
the floor plan, the pattern of bodies, the spilled drinks.
Then there's the Asian group who stakes out the right-
hand corner. Boys who have been taught they aren't
good enough, aren't cute enough for the hot white boys
who surround them. Everyone is watching each other,
besides the old man and the mirror man. Maybe they've
got it all right. Last call. Last scramble to find a match,
a bedmate, someone to lay in the dark with you
for just an hour or two, waiting for the sun to come up.

You know I love you, even though we fight every
other night in this bedroom, where the safety of walls
turns into a steel cage I can't escape, for you hold
all the keys. My mother used to say, *you have to fight
for what you love*, and maybe that's what we're doing:
fighting to love, or is it loving to fight? You know all
the ways to make me hurt, and all the ways to make it
better. Like a doctor with his medic bag, you can cut me
open and put me back together again. Nothing real
has ever happened to us. Nothing so bad. But here

in this room, where I can only see you in slant light,
it feels like everything is crashing down, as if our world
is one large desert with no water, no food, no clothes.
We need a rain dance. Or maybe I'm just a drama queen.
Here we make the pain that keeps us going. Nothing
feels real until you've almost lost it, until you can taste
defeat on your tongue, and you can't imagine doing
anything, but rescuing yourself from the trap you've set,
from the fire that started with the match in your hand.
That's when we give in, fold into the bed, and tell each
other just how lucky we are.

VI.

At his birth, we ask, *will he have a long, happy life? Will he
always love us? Will he know the power of two men together?
Or how hard we had to fight for him? Will he become
the burden we once became to our parents? Will he disappoint?
Will we build his tower too tall?* A voice answers:
If he never knows himself.

                        In the basement, my parents
upstairs, I watch the men on-screen move against
each other, and then the one licks the other in places
I never knew you could be licked.

                                     He is afraid
of his own blood—how it runs through his veins
or down his neck at the prick of the razor. It's blood
that may or may not kill him—may or may not rush
from his body, filling the cracks of a sidewalk.
He lives alone—upstairs apartment built for two.
The men who come and go from his door rarely leave
satisfied for the fear of blood overtakes every moment.
Makes hands nervous, cocks limp, balls full. At night,

he watches men holding hands—strolling the streets.
He imagines how they'll make love in beds flooded
with moonlight, their skin beautiful, their hands
melting into the other, so free, so open—no regret.
In the morning, it's just him, his coffee,
and the newspaper/TV/radio all provoking the fear
in his veins. His blood is marked, is time stamped.

In the tent the lady with cards proclaims I'll have four
children, will marry, will travel with money, or is it travel
for money? She doesn't know, isn't very good at this sort
of thing, is being paid a shitty wage by the fairgrounds,
but she tries, and when she pulls a card she doesn't know,
or doesn't want to read, she slips it into her lap—not
very graceful. My old college roommate once read
my palm on a bored Tuesday night, also said something
about travel and money, nothing about children
or marriage or my death, or about you who stand outside
this tent now, waiting to hear my fortune, my future.
Waiting to know if you will be in it: you, your beauty,
your thick arms that wrap around me, fold me up—
but this she doesn't know as she slips another card
into her already full lap.

                      In that movie with all the sex,
they say 9/11 is the only real thing to ever happen
to our generation, or something like that. Maybe
I'm remembering it all wrong, I do that sometimes.
I was 18 when it happened. 28 now. My adulthood
has been marked, I suppose, by towers that no longer
tower. Tragedy just makes me want to fuck,
which is maybe why that movie has so much
sex in it—real sex, not that Hollywood bullshit.
Who, after fucking, wraps the whole sheet from
the bed around them? Don't you normally just stand

in all your glory? Piss bare-assed, dick out? Hell,
I eat in bed after sex, no sheets in sight. We like
to hide the good parts. The "dirty" parts. A culture
obsessed with sex, yet so afraid of it. I don't remember
the line exactly, maybe it wasn't even important,
but everyone likes to name generations: the lost
generation, the baby boomers, generation X, Y,
and is there a Z yet? What happens next? 9/11
generation sounds so pitiful, as if we're all searching
for help, dialing a number where no one picks up.

VII.

It's Christmas.
The tree is trimmed with silver balls,
red tinsel, a crooked angel.
There's a fire crackling.
It smells of cinnamon and pine needles.
He stands before the tree naked.
In his forties.
His ass is just beginning to lose its battle with gravity.
Winter light is flooding the room.
The year is ending.
Time is rushing by, yet everything feels so slow.
Like this tree that is growing brittle,
sucking water from a tray below.
This tree is holding on to life,
yet knows it's all about to end.
In a week's time, it will be bare, needleless,
and on the corner waiting for the garbage truck
to rumble down the city street in the cold
of a January morning.

THE GHOST OF LITTLE EDIE BEALE
MEETS ME IN A GAY BAR

I spot her by her headscarf: bright rainbow colors
falling onto her barely covered shoulders.

She's at a barstool taking in the bartender in his torn
jeans and leather harness. The lights are dim.

Music is thumping. *Not my kind of music, if you know
what mean?* she whispers against my ear as I order

a drink. We both like rum. *Can you handle this costume?
I felt this was the perfect costume for tonight. What do you think?*

I agree with her as my eyes drift the length of her body,
examining the fabric she's bunched and pinned at her hip—

not a fan of skirts. I promise her she won't see many
tonight—at least not on women. She wants to dance,

but needs space. *Wouldn't mind performing on a stage
in a place like this, with all those beautiful ladies* who I have to

politely explain are really men. Are, in fact, not singing.
Her mother wouldn't approve, but Edie likes the mystery

of it: the world she missed. A world that missed her.
I tell her she's safe here like the man across the bar

wearing his mother's old Sunday dress with hairy legs
and a cheap wig flopping down his face. He'll smoke

cigarettes for the rest of the night, standing right there
with a great view of the bartender's ass, and the dance

floor already covered in sweaty man-on-man action.
Edie's a star here, where gay boys love the eccentric,

the wild, the unbelievable. I tell her there's a beach
out back and her eyes light up. *I could stay on the beach*

for days. But it's dark and this beach is made for cruising,
for hands in bushes, on thighs, a head disappearing

downward then reappearing all smiles and glistening.
She wants to see the beach anyway, wants to feel

the sand on her feet, which may or may not be sanitary.
We walk hand in hand. She's thankful we met.

Says, *where you been all my life?* I shyly remind her
that her life is over, that she died alone in her condo

here in Florida. Her body rotting for nearly five days
before she was found. A quietly tragic way to go,

like my single girlfriend who fears her cats will one day
eat her face after she's fallen in the shower, hit

her head, and bled to death because there was no
one to come home, find her, and save her life.

No white horse. Edie's mouth moves south.
She asks how old I am. *28.* And if I'm married.

Been with a boy for seven years. She nods, *is he good to you?*
I don't believe in divorce. I tell her he is. At the beach,

Edie is quiet. There's the crackling of twigs in the brush,
a flash of man ass. She doesn't notice, but stares out

across the water, the sand curling up between her
painted toes. My eyes drift to the man emerging

from the trees shirtless and out of breath.
That's when she lets out a cry and we both watch

a raccoon scamper across the waterline, make for
the garbage bin behind the bar. She thought she left

her old life behind, *but nothing truly leaves us,* she whispers
as she lifts her hand to her head and rips her scarf off.

It catches in the wind, dances: a rainbow of colors.
Her head is bare, shiny, with little patches of hair

that move in the humid gusts of Florida wind.
Then she dives into the water with barely a ripple.

Barely a sound. Not even the raccoon is startled.

IMAGINING YOUR PENIS IN BLUE
AFTER WATCHING *WATCHMEN*

We could use edible body paint, like the kind our friend
      bought us the year we first fell in love.
We tried it out in our dorm room, slightly turned
      off by the artificial flavoring, the blue blueberry,
or so the packaging claimed. It could transform you
      into a blue god who might glow if placed
in front of the lamp, legs spread: my very own
      superhero. My mouth, suddenly, blue too.

You tolerate my gay boy tendencies to love men in tights,
      capes, or, in Dr. Manhattan's case, completely
naked. You see any movie with me that might titillate
      my geek senses, might awaken a hero.
It's the double-lives, the dorky boys who are really sexy
      and strong and there to save the day that turn me
on. Though Dr. Manhattan was different, so was his penis,
      which the critics couldn't stop talking about:

I don't need some man's penis swinging around in my face. Really?
      Because I can't imagine anything better.
Yes, I'll paint you blue, let you take me to Mars, let us
      watch the world unfold, the straight world
we sometimes feel so disconnected from—only observers.
      Maybe I'll don a Night Owl costume,
for I've always had a soft spot for Patrick Wilson,
      who gave us a slight glimpse of his penis

in *Angels in America*. It wasn't blue and shiny, but beautiful
      all the same. We could make our own movie
where the dorky boy from Indiana is the savior, the one
      with the high-pitched voice who dreams
of fighting crime in the dark of his bedroom. A hero

>   who could've saved the gay man who died
> yesterday in Miami. The one who was attacked last April,
>   but held onto life until October:
>
> the perfect month to die. A gay organization emailed
>   out a picture of him in his hospital bed,
> his little dog there to say goodbye, like our little dog,
>   who curls up between us each night,
> never imagining that one of us could end up beaten
>   and bedridden, beeps of machines keeping
> us alive. And I think of the man at the Pride Festival
>   last weekend with all the black and white
>
> photographs of men and women who have fallen victim
>   to hate crimes. Killed for being the Other.
> He shouted at us each time we walked by, kept repeating
>   *there is a GLBT murder every 9 days*. He said it
> with anger. Said, *you can't ignore it*, but I did. Kept walking.
>   Moving away from the faces staring up at me
> from their graves. I made myself blame them, think they did
>   something wrong that I won't do, which will keep me
>
> alive, keep me from being a face on display meant to haunt
>   gay boy dreams. The truth is my penis isn't blue.
> I have no tights or cape, only fear, and the knowledge
>   that no matter what, humanity is set on destroying itself.

MY FATHER CALLS WITH MORE BAD NEWS

A boy my sister went to high school with killed himself.
How? My father doesn't know, can only read between
the lines of small town gossip and transmit the news
via telephone to me in Florida, far from Midwest tragedy.

Like the closing of another factory, or another farm sold
off, which makes me think of my grandparents' farm
auctioned to the highest bidder, as they stood
in the dirt and watched their possessions disappear

into pickup trucks, loads to be sold on eBay—a concept
they know nothing about. Now they live in town, close
to my parents, in a small house, where my grandfather
finds it hard to walk, to stay on his feet. Often he wakes

in the night, goes to the window expecting to see his fields,
his grape vines, his rundown garage where he spent his days
fixing the broken, breaking the fixed. Now all he sees
is his neighbors' house with their teenage son in the driveway

saying goodnight to a girl, streaked blonde hair. They kiss,
like they've got the rest of their lives, and maybe they do,
or maybe something tragic is looming. Like my best friend
in eighth grade who told me he wasn't going to live past 18,

just had a feeling. This information terrified me—
until he reached 18 and survived. Though his half-brother
nearly died that year, a car accident at 3 a.m., my friend
lucky he didn't go for the late-night food run. And I wonder

if he thinks of telling me this, us huddled at our desks, sharing
boyhood secrets. Or if he thinks of the night he confessed
that his other half-brother was gay and died of AIDS,

and then the night three years later, I told him I was gay,

but wasn't going to die of AIDS, over the phone. Him
at his college up north. Me in college too, but sitting in
Motel 8's parking lot to get a better cell phone signal,
as to not cut out mid-sentence. Now we are both adults

and will continue to grow old, fade away in front
of TV screens. Him watching episodes of *The Twilight Zone*.
Me *I Love Lucy*, like I did every day after school my entire 5th
year as my mother hovered over the fireplace in her gold

sparkly sweater making fire out of old newspapers,
crushed in her hands. On NPR last month they reported
seventeen suicides by young girls all living in the same British
town. The whole place is spooked. A curse? Doomsday?

Or the plot to a really bad horror movie where anyone
with big breasts must die? After hearing the report I turned
to my lover, driving the car, and said, *how strange,
where do you want to eat?* And he answered with no comment

on the girls. The dead girls. Again, I thought it's strange
how tragedy that has nothing to do with us, has so little effect,
no sense of alarm that death is near, is all around.
That we may never again kiss in the driveway late at night

with old men watching, dreaming of snapping beans
on screened-in Indiana porches. The beans fuzzy against hands.
And now my father has reported more tragedy, and I've said,
how's the weather? to change the subject, to ignore the fact

that a boy I once met has killed himself, but there's no ignoring
the question of a suicide note and what it said. The pressure
of a good note would forever keep me alive, revising, worrying
over my last statements to the world, like my last words

to my dad before I hang up the phone and get online to search
for those dead girls. Maybe there's been an eighteenth body,
a discovery of some letter that explains everything (alien
abductions, government plots, terrorism), something I can

tell my father next week when he calls with more bad news.

AGAINST OUR BETTER JUDGMENT
WE PLAN A TRIP TO IRAN

You want to see the spot where they hang boys
for sodomy, want to feel the danger of being two men
together, of being caught in the act, one behind the other.
Tonight we pack our American life into bags marked

"fragile," bags full of books to read on the plane,
our digital camera to record the exotic and the erotic,
and condoms, which you insist we use so we may leave
our mark everywhere we go, a sign of our lust,

which we call love here in our Florida apartment,
where it is almost always sunny. *We'll fuck in every corner
of that goddamn country, in every hotel room, alley way,
bathhouse, and mosque,* your voice erupts from the bathroom,

where you are taking your last shower, your last chance
to "feel clean." You are unmoved by my politically correct
pleas for respect to culture, to a religion that isn't ours to have.
Fuck religion, you say, and I want to agree,

yet fear you long to be hanged, that the martyr in you
is desperate to get out, biting at your ribcage, tearing
at your flesh. Perhaps you want to be a pixilated face
on the TV set: *American Gays Hanged While on Vacation.*

But by morning you'll back out, rip our plane tickets
into pieces, and we'll lie in bed watching CNN,
fucking without condoms until everything burns.

THE ANATOMY OF A HATE CRIME

Setting: Anywhere. Your hometown. Your college town. The place you are visiting. The streets you walk alone or in groups. Alleys where you fuck. Shops where you buy groceries: bananas, tomatoes, boxes of cereal. Or in your bed, just when you think you're safe.

Characters: The victim: That's you, faggot boy. You with that sway in your hips and that lisp in your voice that even the expensive speech therapist couldn't rid you of. Yes, you in that tight-ass t-shirt. You wearing girls' jeans? Did you forget this is a man's world? No room for cocksuckers. Ass eaters. Fudgepackers. The perpetrator: You know who you are. A man's man with a chip on both shoulders, a shitty job, a wife/girlfriend/mother you can't fucking stand. You're stuck. Can't move. There's gum on your shoe and piss in your cup. You think high school was the best motherfucking time of your life. It's over, buddy. But there's a gun in your truck. A knife in your shoe. A baseball bat in your hand.

Action: The hate must be evident. No single gunshot. No clean entry. There must be blunt force. Symbols. Ropes are nice. Tar and feathers if you really want to make a show of it. Give the papers something to write about: *The scene was so gruesome that one has to wonder at the fury and hatred of the killer or killers.* For they will want to believe more than one man did this. As for the victim, he must put up a good fight. Hang on to life for hours upon hours. He is, after all, about to become a martyr. He's seen the stories before, lit candles for other boys, feared he might be next, but never really thought it could happen. He is the heart of the story. Without heart there's no hate.

Conflict: ~~It's born in you to hate the other.~~ Scratch that. We learn hate. But that sounds so preachy, so full of bullshit. There's no rhyme or reason. Is that better? Or worse? No God's punishment. No mental disorder. No drugs or alcohol. Nothing can excuse it, fix it, make it anything, but what it is. But we will write a different tale. One that partially blames the victim, erases a bit of the hate. We need a story that makes sense.

That fits the film running in our minds. A clear beginning, middle, and end. Everything neatly in its place. Here is the body sprawled out, dead, beaten, tear-stained. Here is the killer behind bars. Doing his best white trash sob story. Here are the parents forced into the spotlight, expected to say something of importance, or apologize depending on whose parents they are. Here is the paper outlining the gory details, which will only entertain for so long before the next big news of the day. Here are the gay groups with candles who vow to make things better. Here is the community blamed and dragged through the dirt of *how could this happen*. And here, tucked inside the crowd, are the future victims and killers patiently waiting their turn.

HE DO THE GAY MAN IN DIFFERENT VOICES

Part II

AN EXPERIMENT IN HOW TO BECOME SOMEONE ELSE WHO ISN'T MOVING ANYMORE

The first time we had sex, I didn't know
who would be the top, and who would be
the bottom. The pitcher or the catcher?
The giver or the receiver? I was uneducated

in the ways of men together, was unsure
if you'd given me a signal, so I prepared
for both: ready to take on whatever
you might give, or expect of me.

For you were my first. Before you arrived,
I walked the aisles of a Wal-Mart: the only
shopping location left in our corn-fed,
Indiana town. The local shops shut down

by falling prices and smiley faces. There
I bought condoms, KY Jelly, and blueberry
muffins for the morning after, attempting
to be the dream guy. For I was already madly

in love. I have to say, I was relieved
when you wanted me to top, you to bottom.
We cautiously moved through the motions
that I'd only seen in porn. Passionately

terrified, I overtook your body. Moved inside
you. Felt you all around me as you swallowed
the very center of my maleness. My flesh
as close to your flesh as humanly possible.

Afterward, we laughed at our nervousness,
at our boyhood insecurities, and ate the muffins,

sitting up in bed, our backs propped against
the wall, the crumbs cascading down our torsos,

landing softly in our pubic hair—still wet with first sex.

****

I was born with blond hair.
Like everything it faded.
Faded into red.

****

Jeffrey Dahmer's first two victims were named Steven,
and you remind me that I spell it differently with a "ph."
My parents modeling it after the first Christian martyr,

who was stoned to death. They probably didn't expect
me to be a gay atheist, though in some countries gay men
are stoned to death, atheists too. What a terrible way to die:

one rock at a time. The fury of a mob surrounding you,
teaching their children how to kill, what death looks like,
and just how many stones it takes for a person to crumble,

to give up breath, to no longer move. You think this spelling
difference negates my point, negates my fascination
with Dahmer, who would've liked my gayness, my effeminate

voice, my tight ass, and thick cock. In June of 1978,
I was negative 4-years-old, and Dahmer was just out
of high school. It was the year he took his first victim:

a hitchhiker named Steven. There in his parents' basement
they drank beer, had sex, and when Steven wanted to go,
Dahmer swung a barbell at his head, killing him instantly.

Later he dismembered the body, filled trash bags with pieces
he scattered in the woods behind the house—his parents
never knowing. I understand this fear of leaving—

a body no longer next to you, no longer a part of you,
and you have no idea where they might go, what other bodies
they might discover, and if they'll ever return, like you

return to me each and every night. Tonight, you also remind
me that I've never hitchhiked before, because I was born
in the moment when people began to grow more fearful,

less trusting. When I was two, young boys with blond hair
were disappearing fast. It was all over the news, and my mother
kept dreaming that I'd gone missing, that some man

with perverted ideas had snatched me from my bed, had taken
me to a backwoods cabin where he was fondling my still growing
penis every night, making my little boy body a dumping ground

for his seedy fantasies. She'd wake in the night panicked
and go to my room to see me sleeping soundly to the hum
of a Midwestern winter. The Midwest, where Dahmer

spent most of his life, and where I lived for 22 years before
I escaped to Florida with a boy I loved and still love,
or was he—were you—a man, by then?

****

My students don't understand the poem.

> *Why is it called "Hygiene"?*
> *Why do we have to read it?*
> *Who is Jeffrey Dahmer?*
> *Will there be an exam?*

They are full of questions, and my black
students are full of worry at the line about
black men thinking *it's a treat to get to sleep*

with a white man. Perhaps it's my fault
for beginning the semester with such
a poem, for challenging them in this way.

They want me to stop making them think
of death, the smell of bodies, and hands
unable to get clean. The only serial killer

that interests them is Ted Bundy,
who killed girls on this very campus.
We can see the Chi Omega house,

where the murders took place,
from our classroom window. A man
killing pretty girls is what they like.

It fits their stereotype—everything falls
into place like a badly written and acted
horror flick. They don't care for Dahmer,

or for Reginald Shepherd's version
of events that questions race, sexuality,
and our desires to know someone else.

They don't want to see themselves
in a serial killer, and I don't blame them.
They are young. Life is good. The Florida

sun is hot. The boys on this campus
are Southern gentlemen—no one here
has a secret, a fantasy, an uncontrollable

urge to make everything stop moving.
Or so they believe, as they stare up at me,
wanting me to explain away the poem,

wanting me to make them feel safe
again. Then one, in the back, mutters
under his breath: *serves the faggots right.*

****

Men aren't taught to fear drinks from strangers,
or a ride home, or a promise of sex in a rundown
motel room—a one night stand. Women are taught
to fear all men, are told every man wants to rape
and kill you, and if a man walks behind you
in a parking lot, walk faster, have keys ready,
and be prepared to knee him in the balls—a man's
only weak spot—a woman's only defense.
It's in this gap of fear that men like Dahmer live,
because what man would be afraid of a good-looking
blond man? A white man? A gay man?

****

Black men love the paleness of my body.
        Grow hard at the redness of my hair.
I'm as far from black as you can get.
        It's a treat to get to sleep with a white man.

I could take any of the men in this club home,
        and I have. Have seen my whiteness
sprawled across their darkness—my body stark.
        There is more than sex here,

more than black cock, white ass, red hair between
        legs. We are sleeping with history.

There is a master inside me. A slave inside him.
        There is a white hood under my skin.

Marching feet inside his. We are a symbol:
        two bodies, two races, two men.
We must know how the other feels, smells, tastes.
        The other is exotic, foreign,

though we might've been born on the same
        street in this contemporary America.
Like the beautiful brown man who stood over
        a foot taller than me, and lived down the road.

In the confines of my bed, he moved against me,
        kissed my lips, wanted me to hold him
as he whispered in my ear: *I've never felt so close*
        to another man. A white man. I feared

just how close he wanted to be, our bodies
        already interlocked. We were inches
from the line where pleasure turns to pain,
        where the strong overpowers the weak,

where life slips between the sheets, and a calm
        falls over everything. Then the slow
undoing begins. Self-preservation kicks in.
        No panic. Only action driven

by our need to know what it's like to be
        someone else—someone no longer moving.

****

Milwaukee Incinerates Jeffrey Dahmer's Belongings, 1996

The smell fills the city.

This time of burning.
The melting and crackling
of belongings. The very
things we are made of.
Like the books that pack
the shelves of my apartment,
or my closet full of clothes
I've worn to catch
the attention of a man.
Clothes meant to be removed
quickly, or slowly, depending
on the man. Or my kitchen
full of assorted coffee mugs,
shot glasses, wooden spoons,
and my drawer of knives,
which I never sharpen. Dull
knives are the most dangerous.
They say the greatest punishment
is stripping one of their belongings:
robbery, imprisonment, fire.
Milwaukee is fearful
of the fascination humans have
with things, with stuff,
with the very materials
of our lives. And I think
of the curator on the radio
last month, who had just
been told the lock of Amelia
Earhart's hair, which she had placed
on display at the Women's Air
and Space Museum, was actually
just thread. The history and story
behind it all a lie, and we hate
lies. Hate them so much
that she refused to remove
the thread. It's still on display

with a note explaining how it's not
Amelia's hair, like anything is not
her hair: this piece of thread hanging
from my shirt, or the ball of yarn
that the lady across the street
uses to make baby blankets,
or the string one keeps in a drawer
to tie the legs of a dead chicken
together—stuffed and ready to bake.
We must see the artifacts, real or not.
We must stand in the room
with all the Jews' shoes, must stare
in awe at Napoleon's cot,
must visit the spot where Jesus
was crucified, or where those gay
boys are hanged for sodomy in Iran.
Fact: 400,000 dollars can destroy
history, can destroy the belongings
of a man, can stop the pilgrimage
of people wanting to stand before
Dahmer's refrigerator and breathe
in the pieces of the men
that once lined the shelves. Men
that were once held so tightly
in its door, so tightly in Dahmer's arms.

****

Victim two: Steven, no "ph," not a hitchhiker, but a gay boy
        in a gay club, like I'm a gay boy in a gay club every weekend,
dancing my heart out for the men in tight shirts who stare at me.
        Black men who imagine me naked in their beds,

their cocks inside me. Dahmer found Steven in Club 219 in Milwaukee,
        a club that's now shut down. Steven found Dahmer cute,

charming, and a real gentleman. The police say, Dahmer was a good
    catch and that men described him as being very popular.

A guy you wanted to take home with you. Might even want to date.
    Might one day introduce to your parents. Dahmer took
him to a motel, and I bet they were both hard as they checked in,
    giggling like school girls or young gay boys still spinning

from a night on the town. Eyes still sparkling with alcohol. Ears
    still thumping with music. Once upstairs Dahmer
couldn't resist drugging Steven and having sex with his still body.
    He didn't want to kill him. It had been nine years

since his first kill (the other Steven). He desperately wanted
    to be satisfied by laying next to someone only temporarily
not moving. He wanted to wake in the morning and find
    a still breathing Steven, one he could have breakfast with,

give a good morning kiss, but all he found was Steven's
    severely beaten body. He would never move of his own
accord again. Dahmer had no memory of killing him.
    No memory of Steven's last moments. Had he come to?

Did he know what his fate would hold? Did he fight Dahmer off?
    Did he have any inkling that the man beside him,
the man killing him, would become a serial killer,
    would become famous for this very act,

would become a punch-line to any joke about eating people?
    It wasn't planned, yet Dahmer was calm.
Knew what to do. Left the body. Went to buy a large suitcase.
    Returned and shoved Steven's body inside. Took it

to his grandmother's house, had sex with the corpse in the basement
    while she slept upstairs (why waste a dead body?).
Then he dismembered it, disposed of it, and his second and last

   Steven, without a "ph," was gone forever.

****

I don't tan. I burn.
Fair complexion.
White as snow
falling in Wisconsin.
Or Indiana.
Not Florida.

****

At a Reginald Shepherd Reading, 2006

They say he is sick, almost didn't make it.
I can hear it in his voice and imagine it
in the face of his partner, sitting in the front

row, a head I can only see the back of.
I know it can be hard to love a poet.
To take him in your bed each night,

knowing whatever you do might end up
in his next verse. It is even harder to lose
a poet, or so I imagine. You know all of this

better than I do. You sitting next me
at this reading, your hand on my leg, trying
your best to enjoy this man's poetry.

You do it for me. It is almost holy here.
The windows are stained glass.
There are built-in bookcases everywhere,

and craved ornamentation creeps up

the walls. But out the door and down the stairs
is a dark basement, where my little graduate

cubicle sits, where bodies could hide
for months, because the room always
smells of rotting.

****

There are patterns to everything.
Get up. Go to work. Sit there.
Look productive. Look normal.
Eat lunch with co-workers.
Make small talk. Do not offend.
Smile often (frowning causes
questions). Spend afternoon
staring at computer screen.
Do enough work to not get fired.
Drive home. Cook dinner.
Eat dinner. Have sex with boyfriend
(prove being together for seven
years does not kill your sex drive).
Make boyfriend feel loved. Watch
one hour of television. Brush teeth.
Go to bed with said boyfriend.
Wake in night and shove him
while yelling, *stop snoring*. Go back
to sleep for 2.5 hours. Wake up
and begin again. We are creatures
of habit, of repetition.

Meet black men in gay clubs.
If they are more attractive, promise
them money or free alcohol.
If they are on the same playing
field, promise them sex (a good lay).

Take them home. Offer complementary
beverage laced with drugs. Knock
them out. Make them feel nothing.
Strangle them (it is painless this way).
Have sex with the corpse. Know
what it's like for a body to no longer
move (for a body to take anything
you give it). Masturbate on corpse.
Dismember it. Put the head
and genitals aside for souvenirs
(for safekeeping). Place other pieces
in acid or into bags to be taken
to a landfill or scattered in the woods,
where animals hunt in the dark and
teenagers go to fuck, to feel alive,
to discover their own desires
(their own patterns).

****

Jeffrey Dahmer's Apartment Building is Torn Down, 1992

The leaves have left the trees.
It is November. It is cold
in Milwaukee. A crowd gathers
to watch the wrecking ball
smash into the side
of the building where Dahmer
slept, watched bad TV,
ate takeout, dismembered
bodies, saved souvenirs
in his refrigerator,
took photographs
of the various stages of dying,
of no longer moving.
Bricks are falling.

People are cheering
as if Dahmer will be
the last of his kind,
but there will always be men
with fascinations, with desires,
with patterns, and boxes under
their beds, treasures in their closets,
fingernail clippings under
their bathroom sinks.
This building can crumble,
can fall to the ground,
a 7-Eleven can go
up in its place, or a movie rental
store, or a pawn shop,
but people will always know
this is the spot where Dahmer killed
those men. And on Halloween
teenagers will gather to try
and convince each other
that those men are whispering
to them, telling them
what it feels like to die,
to stop moving,
but that is for another year,
another time. For it is November.
The leaves are gone from
the trees. It is cold
in Milwaukee. And a building
is falling down.

****

You worry I'm imaging him
when I lie on top of you
and beg you to put one hand
around my throat, and one hand

on my dick. I want you to push
into my neck, to almost stop
my breath. I want you to show me
that you could end it all right here
in this wrought-iron bed,
in this little apartment,
in this state of heat.
It is the pleasure that walks up
to pain that makes me so thankful
to be alive, to be in your arms,
to know everything is fleeting.

****

15 consecutive life sentences
45 years of Reginald Shepherd
957 years in prison
34 years of Jeffrey Dahmer
7 years of you and me together
27 years of Stephen with a "ph"

****

I wonder if Dahmer ever flipped
      through his TV in the 1980s
and saw *Today's Special*, a kids' show
      about a mannequin named Jeff
who comes to life each night with the help
      of his magic hat. If so, did he fear
the mannequin he stole from a Milwaukee
      department store would, one night,
suddenly breathe, sit up, and ask him,
      why me, Jeffrey? It helped to satisfy
his urge to kill. He'd masturbate on it,
      and imagine real men—
not moving. That is until his grandmother
      found it and made him throw it out.

Mannequins terrify normal people.
  As a kid, I longed for each one I saw
to jump from his pedestal just like Jeff
  with his magic hat, and to tell me
all the secrets to a life that both moves
  and stops. I wanted all of them
to be my friends, my companions—
  like Dahmer's collection of heads—
skulls eventually. An audience that could
  watch him, love him, but never
leave him.

****

How many lives does a gay man have?
How many shots?
How many strangers' houses have I entered
looking for a hot fuck?
How many times have I survived?
All of them.
No one stopped me from moving.
No one stopped me from leaving.
How close have I come to being a head
and a penis on a shelf in a refrigerator?

****

The city hasn't stopped.
Every blond man
looks like him. Every
white man could be him.

****

Reginald Shepherd is Dead, 2008

I wake in the night and reach for your body, a body

I've grown so accustomed to after five years
together. I feel the flesh of your arm. I lay my hand
on your chest just to feel the beat of your heart,
to know that I'm not alone in this world just yet.

Cancer. It was a long, hard battle with that word
that seems to be everywhere. Not getting cancer
is the rarity these days, these long days in Florida
where Reginald also lived. It is September
and the leaves are beginning to fall in Indiana,

where you and I both grew from little boys to strong
men, where we first discovered the touch of another
man, another body. At 25, I am still young. You
are even younger. We have a life ahead of us.
More love to make. More poems to write.

More times to lay skin to skin. But I know that one
of us will lose the other. One of us will see the other's
body no longer moving, and I selfishly hope it's you,
because your body moves so beautifully,
and I never want to see it stop.

****

We dress as zombies for Halloween—the living dead.
We pose in pictures, our faces pale, our eyes sunken
by dark makeup. We do the standard zombie arms
stretched in front of us, then the *Thriller* hands.
We still move around the apartment. We still laugh
with friends, and later we head to a gay club and dance
as zombies in the darkened disco, bodies all around.

Dahmer wanted to create the living dead—a body
that was his to control, one he could have for all time.
It never worked. He claims just one victim remained
in and out of consciousness for two days after he drilled

holes in his brain and filled them with acid. Everyone else died quickly. It was a failed experiment in how to control the nearly living, the barely moving.

****

Jeffrey Dahmer is Killed in Prison, 1994

November is the cruelest month,
if you are Jeffrey Dahmer.
Leaves fall. It is cold.
He was just 34 when the black
prisoner bashed his head in
with a broomstick. It seems a fitting
end for a man who loved black men,
loved watching them grow still.
I wonder if Dahmer had a second
to appreciate just how perfect
an ending this was. No one
could've written it better.
As he fell onto the dirty prison tile,
I wonder if he saw the faces of the 17
men he killed. I wonder if the Stevens
were there in his head, his first two
killings, or maybe he was past
all that. Maybe all he could think
about was God, for he had found
religion in prison as many do
when faced with the silence
of a steel box, and I, too, was religious
in 1994 at the age of 12. Dahmer
gained religion, and I lost it.
November can be a quiet month.
The birds head South. The leaves
pile at the end of Midwestern
driveways, where boys run in woods.
Boys who don't understand

the fascination they have with death,
with everything in life that moves
and then, eventually, stops.

HE DO THE GAY MAN IN DIFFERENT VOICES

Part III

IN A PORN STORE

I stand here searching
      for your videos,
           for your body
of work. Something to make me
      whole again.

They say the center cannot hold,
      that two men will fall apart,
           that we are all going to hell.
    Even you,
           because *once you fuck a man,*
              you're gay forever,
and bashing old people doesn't help either.

Boxes line the shelves promising
      raw, nasty boys,
      big, thick cocks,
      tight asses,
but I want you.

You in *Latinolicious*,
      even though you aren't Latino,
or in *Code Violators*,
      which seems a fitting label for us both.
It's also the one where you fuck
      the redheaded boy,
           red like me.

Or *Big Dick Club 2* because one
      wasn't big enough,
           and *Proven Straight*
where you showcase your "straightness"
           by fucking lots of hot boy ass.

In the sale bin they have *Just Add Water*,
        our first film. I pick it up,
                run my finger over your face,
      remembering the first time I came
while watching you.

      Edmon, I want you to believe me
when I say I'm sorry,
        sorry for what's to come,
                sorry for both of us.

THERE IS NO NICKOLAY PETROV

Nickolay is the man I watch fucking on my 46" TV.
        The guy who can make me hard with one
look, one flex, one cumshot.

Edmon is the man who sits in his cell writing me letters.
        Makes and sells greeting cards, so he can buy
stamps. Says he writes only to his mother and me.

Nickolay is a rising star. Porn execs can make him
        into anything exotic: Russian, Latino, straight.
He uses his accent to command beautiful twinks.

Edmon is on the basketball league in prison, works
        in the kitchen, reads *USA Today*, says his
family knows nothing of his porn past.

Nickolay is a hot commodity, sells lots of DVDs,
        magazines, gets millions of hits on websites,
could have a long successful career.

Edmon keeps busy. Is taking guitar lessons, enjoys
        my poetry. He writes a little himself,
but is too embarrassed to share it.

Nickolay has won a GAYVN award for best threesome
        in his film *Just Add Water*. This is the first
scene I saw of his, a scene I now watch on repeat.

Edmon is Armenian, came to the U.S. in 2004,
        is bisexual, says in his country you can't be
open about your sexuality, about your lifestyle.

Nickolay has a perfect porn dick and can use it well.
        His bottoms often say, *he fucks with the blank
intensity of an animal.* He really knows how to plow.

Edmon says I'm a good-looking guy, wonders if I
        have a boyfriend. I tell him I do. I read
good-looking guy over and over. I can't stop smiling.

Nickolay is a top—only. Has no plans to bottom,
        often plays straight until proven gay.
I say give him time. Give him money.

Edmon misses the thump of the music, the heat
        of the dance floor, the smell of sweat
on skin. I tell him I go dancing every weekend.

Nickolay takes $5,000 to beat up an old couple who
        owes some guy money. He attacks them
three times between September 2006 and April 2007.

Edmon once lived down the street from my apartment
        here in Florida. Says he knows exactly where I am,
can picture it from his cell in Louisiana.

Nickolay dresses as a deliveryman for the first attack,
        sounds like the beginning of a porn.
This one ended with a hammer to a head.

Edmon got hired as a go-go dancer at the club
        I go to every week. Says he never showed up
to work. Never had a chance. Everything is about timing.

Nickolay is arrested in January 2008, in Florida,
        for attempted murder. Later it's revealed
he was considering killing the couple for $10,000.

Edmon has gained more muscle, more definition,
        since entering prison, has little else to do.
Says the porn execs would beg to have him back.

Nickolay admits during the trial *I was trying to prove*
        something, I guess. News reports claim
he showed little to no remorse.

Edmon is surprised by my letters. Says he didn't
        know if his fans remembered him.
Didn't know he won an award for best threesome.

Nickolay doesn't exist beyond the reach of my
        screen. He is a fantasy. My fantasy.
A man inside another man.

Edmon is Nickolay. Says I can call him either.
        After my second letter I pick Edmon.
Edmon is real. Edmon is serving 20 years.

SEPTEMBER 21, 1991

Armenia didn't have a wall. No great televised moment,
        no David Hasselhoff to sing, no symbol to destroy.
It was lackluster. A vote. Done. In September of 1991,
        I was eight years old and sitting in a third grade classroom:
plastic seats, metal desks, all arranged in small circles.

You were six, heard your mother and father whispering
        about independence, about possibility.
I wonder if it was then that you first envisioned
        America—freedom. I think of you as that boy:
small, innocent with beautiful skin and dark hair,

just a touch of curl to it, and I with my light hair.
        I was blond at eight, not yet a redhead, for my hair
wouldn't darken until I turned eleven. I, too, was innocent
        that September, little did I know that in just six
months I'd experience my first death. My grandmother

would collapse on a cold Sunday in February. My parents
        rushing to her house, leaving my sisters and me
huddled together in the basement, knowing there
        was something to fear, but what? I can still see
my parents' faces standing in the doorway, framed in wood

paneling. Their eyes cloudy. Death had found us.
        Our lives were never going to be
the same. Like yours changed when you left Armenia, came
        to this country, got discovered, got caught up
with the wrong crowd. How you packed that bag,

went to New York City, dressed as a deliveryman, knocked
        on that couple's door, and fractured their skulls
with a hammer. I want to send my eight-year-old self

    to Armenia in 1991. I want him
to find you sitting in your room, listening to your parents

talk of freedom, of independence from the Soviets. Yes,
    I want to creep into your room at night,
whisper in your ear all the things that will go wrong,
    warn you of all the moments you'll regret.
I want to rewind the tape, unpack the bag, return

to the beginning, to the moment when everything felt
    possible, before death, before prison when we
were just boys. Boys who could grow up and become anything.

JUST ADD WATER, **SCENE 2**

When you appeared on screen I was already hard
        from the cute twinks sucking each other off.
I didn't expect you. Didn't expect your dark eyes
        or accented commands: *now fuck him*
in the ass, yeah like that! I was sitting on the couch,
        my boyfriend next to me, he too is dark haired.
Our breath was full of the alcohol from the bar
        where we got a free copy of your DVD,
some erotica night. A night we almost took another guy
        home with us, but settled for the familiar
and a threesome on DVD. It was there I fell for you,
        fell for your perfectly toned body, your cock,

and that cumshot; how far it went, reminding me
        of my boyfriend in the first year
we were together, when everything was new,
        when he would shoot his cum over his head
and onto my dorm room walls and carpet.
        How it always made me feel primal—alive.
In bed that night, still swaying from rum, I dreamt
        you came to me, entered me: a place I won't
let anyone go. As you leaned in, I caught your eyes,
        eyes that said: *nothing lasts forever.*

$5,000

My first car didn't cost $5,000, more like $1,500. It was the car
        I drove to school each day. The one I nearly crashed
that winter when the Indiana roads filled with ice and I hit

the guardrail, a far drop into a gorge on the other side, where
        on summer days I'd search for trilobites and Indian
heads. But I managed to correct myself, just minor scrapes

to the side door. I was 17. My first job I made just over $5,000
        in one year. Worked as a book boy at the public
library. Walked between the stacks, got lost in the smell of paper,

of spines, of binding. There I first imagined being a writer.
        Having books of my very own that some boy
would get paid minimum wage to shelve. I quit to go to a college

that cost $5,000 times four each year. It was there, in the winter
        of my sophomore year, that I first whispered *I'm gay*.
Wrote confessions in a journal as I sat in my car facing the Ohio

River, watching barges go by in the bleak landscape. Then I'd drive
        back to campus past the historic buildings. The ones
with the mark of the last flood, and I'd long for another one,

just to see all that water and destruction. Later, that same year,
        I went to Europe with a ticket that cost nearly $5,000,
round-trip. Spent two months walking the streets of Dublin,

where I imagined skinny boys with funky haircuts following me
        back to my bed where we would discover each other's smell.
It never happened. Not even with the dark-haired boy who worked

at a clothing shop I walked by daily. A boy I stared at with intensity,
> who never returned the look. Months later, back
in the States, I found a boy, an Indiana boy, who returned

all my looks. We fell in love and moved to Florida where boys
> parade in tiny swimsuits and my boy confessed
he had $5,000 in credit card debt, which he had used to woo me,

to buy me tickets to shows, take me to expensive dinners, buy me
> gifts. I was angry, yet flattered. I was 23; he was just 20.
So many things you can do with $5,000, so many ways to get it.

MY BOYFRIEND TELLS MY PARENTS I'M WRITING
TO A GAY PORN STAR IN PRISON

Immediately, it's about violence. Somehow writing to a prisoner
        is condoning their actions, as if I'm encouraging the world
to make gay porn and beat up the elderly for money.

I'm defensive of my actions. Protective of this man I barely know.
        A man I'm hoping will give me some reason to believe
in him. A reason I'm so interested. I pull out my liberal "stand up

for prisoners' rights" speech and one on "racial and ethnic bias
        in the justice system." I mention how he got 20 years
for assaulting a couple three times, and others get less for killing

children, for raping women, for murdering gays. My parents will bend
        to my way of thinking in the course of our discussion,
but will go home saying, *our son is obsessed with porn and convicts,*

what happened to being happily gay and coupled? To bring it home I mention
        my artistic project, my poetic bending of the truth, my need
for material, and perhaps it's this that makes me so defensive.

The guilt that comes from using his letters, his stories, his actions.
        The guilt I feel with every word I write. By the end my mother
is patting my shoulder and telling me *it's okay, I look forward to seeing*

what you write, and I'm standing there like Truman Capote telling
        the world how amazing my book will be if they'd just kill
those men. Hang them, so I can have my ending.

LINES FROM A PRISON LETTER

It's very nice to hear from someone on the outside.
        Nice to know there's still people
who appreciate what I did in the "modeling" business.
        The prison here is not bad, nothing
like they show in the movies. It's peaceful.
        Please send me your picture. I'm sure you
can get pictures of me in any position you want,
        anytime you want. I heard that people
with red hair have a very high sex drive.
        I bet it's true in your case.
What are your hobbies (other than enjoying
        my performances)? Your letter smelled
so good. I miss cologne. Where I am from you
        can't tell people you're gay or that you've
had sexual experiences with other guys.
        They will kill you.
That's why I learned to act like a macho guy,
        play sports, work out. When I first
got to prison, no one wrote to me or returned
        my calls. I was left with a sense of loneliness,
a sense of abandonment. I like that it's so busy here.
        I have a job. I'm learning guitar.
Please tell your boyfriend not to be jealous
        that we write to each other, after all
we're just friends. Are you disappointed
        that I like women as well as men?
I just like life, like to enjoy all the pleasures
        it has to offer. I have to tell you
I liked your poems very much. You're very
        talented. It's cool that your work
has been published in magazines. Send me one.
        Write me more about yourself.

Do you have siblings? Where are you originally
      from? When did you first discover
you were gay and how did it feel? It's interesting
      to read intimate and personal stories
from strangers. I'm very open-minded
      and don't judge others. Sorry
if I'm getting too deep. Take care of yourself,
      and I hope to hear from you soon.
Your favorite star, Edmon

$10,000

The car in front of me has magnetic advertisements
        announcing bank-owned properties starting at $10,000.
This is a recession they say on the news every single day.
        Unemployment is at 10%. I hate my job, but fear losing it.

I make four times $10,000 a year. More money than I've ever
        made in my life, and I think of my friend in high school
who once said he couldn't possibly make under $100,000
        and had to select his career based on this need.

Clearly, he didn't get an English degree like me. I didn't tell him
        that my parents made less than that—put together.
My credit card has a $10,000 credit limit and I have $9,942.68
        charged on it, because I was unemployed for six months,

because I have a master's degree in creative writing. I have even more
        in school loans. My friend wonders if she can pay
for her wedding with $10,000 or less. I tell her I can't get married,
        so I don't really know, which means, I guess, I don't really care.

My boyfriend and I have spent nearly $10,000 on drinking and tipping
        drag queens in the last year and a half,
because when you're in debt and hate your job and hear every day
        on the radio that things might get worse, there's nothing

better to do than drink, dance, and stick dollar bills in a sweaty drag
        queen's hand or down some man's g-string.
Am I exaggerating? Possibly. In college, I helped raise a tenth
        of $10,000 for an AIDS organization in Louisville, Kentucky.

It felt good to know I had done something for someone,
        that I had played the role of savior. According to the U.S.
Department of Justice, it costs a little over $10,000 per prisoner
        per year in Louisiana. This is one of the cheapest places

in the United States to be in prison. Some still think it costs too much.

I TELL EDMON HE WRITES BETTER THAN MY STUDENTS

And they aren't in prison, aren't former porn stars
          (at least I don't think). Edmon worries
because I teach writing that I'll judge his misspellings
          and awkward grammar. English is his third

language, which reminds me how stupid Americans
          can be. I took French for six years and still
can't speak it or write it, can barely read it.
          My students have it easy, sitting at their little

desks with their brand new laptops, groaning when I ask
          them to write a four-page essay about
themselves. I want to tell them I have a friend in prison,
          a former gay porn star, and he writes more

than that in one letter. I want them to read his letters,
          want them to know the American Dream
doesn't always work out. Most of them will fail,
          will never become the artists they envision

themselves to be, some will end up in prison like Edmon,
          others tied to a job they hate, a wife and kids,
and when they turn 40 they'll fuck some young piece
          of ass, because there never seemed to be

another option. Yes, Edmon writes better than
          these 18-year-old kids who tell me of drug
addiction. One boy writing how at 16 he was spending
          over $1,000 on crack a month. I write

in the margins of his paper: *I need more information. How*
        does a 16-year-old have that kind of cash?
I got 20 bucks every two weeks as an allowance
        in high school. I should thank my parents

for not giving me enough money to become an addict.
        Another tells me of gangs in New Orleans,
of life after Katrina, but I think he's seen too many movies.
        He thinks his white teacher wants to envision him,

a young black man, as the boy who got out, as the boy
        education can save, because in Hollywood
white ambitious teachers are the only ones who can save
        black kids from gangs, violence, their own families,

maybe even hurricanes. White as savior: I'm not buying it,
        nor would Edmon, who has seen the white man
as con artist, as power hungry, as a porn exec
        who no longer cares, or writes, or calls.

Yes, there are only so many stories I can read
        about childhood tragedies, drunk driving
accidents, bad middle school breakups. My students
        are young and would be shocked that I think

a gay porn star in prison writes better than them.
        But that's life. It never turns out the way
we plan. Life is me sitting in my cubical scrawling
        on papers: *this was a good topic for an essay,*

but remember to include details, capitalize "I", and indent
        your paragraphs. Or it's Edmon in his cell, listening
to the slamming of doors, and writing to me: *I got involved*
        with the wrong crowd, and now I'm paying for it.

A HISTORY OF BLOOD

Another gay boy got bashed in Miami this week, nearly beaten
        to death on his way home from a club. The man's fist
smashed the boy's glittered face, like my glittered face dancing

at the gay bar every weekend, waiting for my dark shadow
        to appear, my messenger of death to jump out shouting
faggot over and over again until it sounds like gibberish, not even

a real word, meaning a bundle of sticks bound together and used
        as fuel. The media will ask: *what did this gay boy do
to deserve such a beating?* Because he must have done something,

and even I, in all my gayness and liberalism, will wonder if he called
        out to the guy in a drunken come-on or if he provoked
him by acting extra faggy, by pushing all the buttons of petrified

heterosexual males, who only know the power of fists, sticks,
        stones, not even guns, unless used backward, barrel
to face. Danger runs in our gay blood. Blood that makes me write

letters, sprayed with cologne, to a man in prison, a man who beat
        an elderly couple, fractured their skulls not once,
but three times. A man with broad shoulders, muscled arms,

a chiseled chest. A man who makes me hard because he could kill
        me, could take my life and end it. It's the same blood
that got Matthew in that truck with those two boys, the blood that

later ran down his face while coyotes howled in the distance,
        and it's the blood of Capote in Perry's cell, cold blood
that's seen men carried away in paddy wagons, hands over faces,

men who've felt the thrust of nightsticks in stomachs or ropes
          around necks. It's the blood in my veins that makes me
write *fag* on my arm in neon green body paint and go out searching

the streets for men who can't control their fascination with boys
          whose bodies scream: *you wanna kill me, don't you.*
    Fearless boys with glitter in their blood.

I DREAM EDMON ESCAPES

He digs a tunnel from his cell to the other side
        like Andy in *The Shawshank Redemption*, except
he isn't innocent. It's steamy hot in Louisiana
        when he triumphantly emerges
in the swampy landscape as a free man, ripping away
        his prison garb, pounding on his rock-hard
chest. He hitchhikes to the nearest town, blowing
        the truck driver as payment, as any good porn star
would do. In return he gets enough money to buy new
        clothes and take a Greyhound to Orlando,
to my apartment. The one he knows about from his past life,
        once living close by. He can picture me
sitting here on the balcony, the sway of palm trees,
        the Florida breeze in my red hair. He arrives at dark,
lights out, me in my tight underwear and nothing else.
        He knocks on the door with force. The kind of knock
you can't ignore for fear of the whole door collapsing
        beneath one fist, unlike the Jehovah's Witnesses
who knock lightly, secretly hoping the gay couple won't answer.
        I open the door, take in his flesh, his face,
his body. This a man I've only seen on TV screens,
        computer monitors, a man I've imagined over and over
again. Here he stands in my silly Florida apartment
        with my books lining the shelves, my little dog jumping
at him, my old kitchen table in the corner, originally
        my grandmother's, the one who died that February
morning all those years ago. Edmon looks me in the eye,
        moves toward me in slow motion, because it's my dream,
and I want to take it all in: every movement he makes
        as he wraps his thick arms around me, even buffer
from the prison gym. He tells me he's waited all his life
        for this moment and then we kiss like one of us

has been void of affection for too long. I pull at his clothes
        and he slides down my underwear, wanting flesh
on flesh. His stomach to mine. His dick brushing my dick.
        Here on the floor, beneath the dusty fan, we make love
with the moonlight on our skin. Inside me, he whispers,
        everything will be okay as long as we've got each other.
In the morning, we're just two men on the run, two men
        in disguise: fake mustaches, a bottle of hair dye,
two pair of reading glasses. He promises to protect me
        from the flashing lights, from the men in uniform
climbing the stairs as we leap out the open window, hoping
        for the best this life has to offer.

SITTING IN MY CUBICAL
I RECONSIDER A PORN CAREER

I could still use my teaching skills, could play
the part of the young English instructor, or tutor,
who must teach his students how to take cock,
eat ass, give head. How to earn that A. It would
be more fun than sitting here under bad lighting,
grading paper after paper after paper. Florida
is full of gay porn studios and when I first moved
here, jobless for months, I almost did it. Almost
called them up, almost sent them pictures,
which I took one lazy afternoon, the July sun
seeping into my living room where I attempted
to make my dick look as big as possible, my ass
firmer, my stomach more toned. I've got the red
hair that guys find exotic, the slim body, and the cute
boy smile. I even posted an ad on Craigslist
for naked maid service. Got ten replies in the first
hour—but never went through with it. Never
showed up at some balding man's condo
with a bucket of supplies and rip-away pants. Never
let him follow me around as I bent and scrubbed
his floors, folded his laundry, washed his dishes.
It was a line I wouldn't cross, but now sitting here,
using my fancy degree, I can't think of anything
better than fucking for money, and who cares what
the world thinks? Edmon says the porn industry
has its dark sides, but he has no regrets.
There's something courageous about men
pounding away at each other under hot studio lights.
The director stopping them every few minutes
to get all the right angles. The catering staff laying
out sandwiches. An HR guy writing checks.
An errand boy buying more condoms and lube.

These are the scenes I illegally download and watch
with my dick in hand, thinking of Edmon,
of how in a different life we could have met
on a set, where he would've been asked to fuck me
by a man with a camera shouting *action* while
choking down another ham and cheese on rye.

AFTER WATCHING *CAPOTE* I DECIDE NOT TO SEND THESE POEMS TO EDMON

Perry asked Capote, *what is the name of your book?*
        after seeing the clipping in *The New York Times*
about Capote reading from his new work: *In Cold Blood*.
        Such a great title, that is unless it's your blood
that's cold. Those men died never reading Capote's
        version of their lives, of their one life-changing
decision, and I think of Edmon in his cell reading
        these poems, seeing his life on the page, cut
and spliced with my own life. Would he understand
        my interest? Know that I never meant to judge
him, or state what is right or wrong, that part of me cares
        for him, doesn't want to see him hurt?
I never told him about the poems, and now it's too late.
        He might think I've been a fake all this time,
that my only motivation was writing and becoming famous.
        He doesn't know that poets can't become famous
anymore, that only a handful of people will ever read
        these, some to get off on them, others to point
out the academic in me: the techniques, references, style.
        Others will hate me for writing such trashy poems,
for discussing porn, cum, hard-ons, and for constantly
        writing about writing poems in the poems.
Fame will not be mine. Edmon, a gay porn star and prisoner,
        will always be more famous than me. *What is the name
of your book?* Could I lie? Could I go visit Edmon, stand
        in his cell, bring him books to read, and lie to him
about my own? Would we grow close? Would the guilt
        eventually overtake me? Would we ever share
a kiss? Both caught in the moment, our lives sliding past
        each other, like the cell door closing. Capote and me
on the outside. Perry and Edmon forever on the inside.

YOU'VE GONE SILENT

I search the porn blogs for news of your death,
thinking they'd, at least, devote a blurb to you,
if you, in fact, have died in prison. I imagine
a fellow inmate discovering your gay-porn past,
making you pay for it in the shower every night,
then one night taking it too far: ending your life.
Perhaps I've watched too many episodes of *Oz*,
or too much porn, that this is my first guess
at your whereabouts. But even I, who enjoy forceful
sex, don't want to see you demeaned, forced
down, ass ripped open, pleading for your life.
You have such a perfect ass, one that needs cared
for softly, gently. I guess, it could have been simpler:
accidently stabbed in a fight that didn't involve you,
because in prison everyone is guilty. Everyone
worthy of a knife to a stomach. Maybe it was bad
food, poor medical treatment, swine flu, or maybe
I'm just ignoring the reality that you've stopped
writing me and are still alive. Still breathing.
Still sitting in your cell learning guitar, making
greeting cards, writing poems you won't show me.
I might prefer you dead, and yes, I'm a little
embarrassed to say so, a little guilty, but it's been
months, and nothing, not a word. I thought you
loved my letters. Didn't find me creepy or annoying.
I thought we could be friends, pen-pal lovers.
Edmon, I want you dead or alive, I just need
to hear from you.

IMAGINING YOU IN A PRISON PHOTOGRAPH

"Behind every anonymous number, a very specific face," –C. D. Wright

When I think of you there, all I see is grayness; a bleak
        figure against the swampy landscape of Louisiana.
My mind jumps decades. It isn't 2010 in prison. It is the 1930s.
        '40s. '50s. You are there in a tight white t-shirt.
Your cigarettes rolled in your sleeve. You're leaning against
        a fence, pretending not to care about the confines of wire,
about the photographer trying to create something true,
        something real. A face in the bleakness.

You wear striped gray pants that hug your ass and groin
        in all the right places. You are beautiful—and know it.
There, in the prison yard, the grass worn thin from men walking
        in circles, you think of your homeland. Your mother
sitting by the window writing you letters. Her hand shaky.
        Her pen nearly out of ink. She knows where you are,
but is unsure how you got there. How you got from her home,
        where she cooked for you, read to you, taught you
how to be a good man, to that tiny steel box in a country
        she doesn't know, a land she doesn't understand.

Then I imagine you turning toward the camera and thinking
        of me and the letters you hold to your nose fantasizing
about the redheaded poet who wrote them, sprayed them,
        laid his lips upon them. The poet sitting in Florida,
where spring will soon begin. It is in this moment
        that the photographer presses the button, the shutter
snaps shut, and you are captured.

NOTES

"Warning: In Case of Rapture This Vehicle Will Be Unmanned": This poem is dedicated to the memory of Michael Miller, Drew Chapin, and Jill Caputo.

"Iranian Boys Hanged for Sodomy, July 2005": This poem refers to the event that occurred on July 19, 2005, when two young men (one rumored to be 16) were publically hanged in Iran for the crime of sodomy. They were held in prison for 14 months where they were beaten until they confessed to having gay sex. An estimated 4,000 lesbians and gay men have been put to death in Iran since 1979 when the ayatollahs took power. The incident was reported in *The Advocate*, July 2005.

"He Do the Gay Man in Different Voices": The title of the poem is a play off the original title of T. S. Eliot's "The Waste Land" ("He do the Police in Different Voices"). Sections of the poem are also inspired by the website *Visual AIDS* and in particular their gallery called "The Damaged Narcissist" published in December of 2005.

"An Experiment in How to Become Someone Else Who Isn't Moving Anymore": The title of this poem and the line "it's a treat to get to sleep with a white man" are from Reginald Shepherd's poem "Hygiene."

ACKNOWLEDGEMENTS

I want to thank the following publications for first printing the poems below:

"A History of Blood." *New Mexico Poetry Review.* Spring 2011 Issue. "Against Our Better Judgment We Plan a Trip to Iran." *Knockout.* Issue 3, Spring 2010. "My Father Calls With More Bad News." *Pank Magazine.* Issue 4.2, 2009. "Iranian Boys Hanged for Sodomy, July 2005." Winner of the 2008 Gival Press Oscar Wilde Poetry Award and published in the anthology *Poetic Voices Without Borders: 2*, 2008. "Warning: In Case of Rapture This Vehicle Will Be Unmanned." *Chelsea Station.* Issue 1, November 2011. "Sex Education." *Pank Magazine.* Issue 7.2, 2012.

My deepest gratitude goes to Dr. Kathy Barbour for her vast knowledge, encouragement, and humor. I'm also deeply thankful to the faculty of Florida State University where I earned my MFA. Special thanks goes to Dr. David Kirby who taught me more than he will ever know and to Erin Belieu who could always find my weakest line and make me realize I could do better.

I have endless thanks and admiration to my Black Tarp comrades: Brianna Noll, Derek Phillips, Peter Alvarez, and Stephanie Singletary. All of you inspired me to constantly out do myself.

I'm also thankful for the support of my family and my Orlando friends who have kept me going these last three years. Special thanks go to Alex Rister and Jeremy Halinen for their careful eyes. I'm also thankful to my friend Annie Simkin for her belief in me for so many years.

Thanks to Bryan Borland for his constant support and to all the poets who have inspired me in one way or another.

Finally, much love and thanks to Dustin Carter who helped make each one of these poems possible.

ABOUT THE PUBLISHER

The mission of Sibling Rivalry Press is to develop, publish, and promote outlaw artistic talent - those projects which inspire people to read, challenge, and ponder the complexities of life in dark rooms, under blankets by cell-phone illumination, in the backseats of cars, and on spring-day park benches next to people studying Frank O'Hara and Mina Loy. We welcome manuscripts which push boundaries, sing sweetly, or inspire us to perform karaoke in drag. Not much makes us flinch.

www.siblingrivalrypress.com

ABOUT THE POET

Stephen S. Mills has an MFA from Florida State University. His poems have appeared in *The Gay and Lesbian Review Worldwide, PANK Literary Magazine, The New York Quarterly, The Antioch Review, The Los Angeles Review, Knockout, Assaracus, Mary,* and others. He is also the winner of the 2008 Gival Press Oscar Wilde Poetry Award. This is his first book.

www.stephensmills.com

www.ingramcontent.com/pod-product-compliance
Lightning Source LLC
LaVergne TN
LVHW041342080426
835512LV00006B/580